Butte, Montana, copper mines, 1892.
Photographer unknown.

Opposite page:
Free flowing well, Nebraska, 1885.
Photographer, Silas Melander.

The Taming of
THE WEST

A Photographic Perspective

Compiled & Edited By
DAVID R. PHILLIPS

WITH COMMENTARY BY
ROBERT A. WEINSTEIN AND DAVID R. PHILLIPS

HENRY REGNERY COMPANY · CHICAGO

Library of Congress Cataloging in Publication Data

Phillips, David R   1931-
    The Taming of the West.

    1. Frontier and pioneer life—The West—Pictorial
works.   2. The West—History—Pictorial works.
I. Title.
F596.P47   917.8'03'0222   74-6903
ISBN 0-8092-8402-2

To the memory of the photographers who made this book
possible—E. E. Henry, Harrison Putney, Horace Stevenson,
Joseph E. Smith, Silas & Lewis Melander, N. A. Forsyth,
B. W. Kilburn, and the unknown photographers.

Design by Robert Carey.

Thanks for invaluable assistance to
Ric Clark, Linda Foerster, and Gary George.

Left:
Marie Baehl, Leavenworth, Kansas, circa 1880.
Photographer, Harrison Putney.

Below:
Stereoscopic card illustration.
Photographers, Silas & Lewis Melander, Chicago, 1876.

Opposite page:
William F. Cody, circa 1895.
Photographers, Burke & Koretke, Chicago.

iv

Contents

Washing machine, circa 1900.
Photographer, Horace Stevenson, Leavenworth, Kansas.

Minnesota log jam, circa 1890.
Photographer unknown.

Introduction

Whole stories are rarely told. The process of living is a process of selection, and what men most often select to endure are but carefully chosen fragments of history. In the scale of recording the history of men's efforts, the photograph, particularly the nineteenth-century photograph, has won for itself a high level of believability. It is widely accepted now, even as it was then, as a faithful witness of what the camera has been directed to see, and no more. This reproduced selection of photographs is an opportunity to see in that respect what those who lived when these photographs were made thought valuable, useful, challenging, exciting, questioning, and demanding. To put a finer point on it, we are seeing what many individual photographers, each imprisoned by his environment, his experiences and outlook, thought was important to preserve. Knowing this, we must accept, therefore, that what we are able to see on these pages is only a small, subjective fragment of a larger truth that may forever escape us. Yet these fleeting images have enduring meaning, for they suggest, as the shadow suggests the substance, the existence of a complex, fascinating panorama of human endeavor and human foolishness. These photographs, never before published, are a vivid offering, a part of the immense tale of the efforts to transform a prairie wilderness into the teeming, industrial colossus of the present-day United States.

The photographers who made these pictures range from the professional, with his pressing commercial requirements to make a living, to the itinerant,

who photographed largely for the pleasure of capturing and mastering a new skill or a new piece of equipment. Even these itinerants hoped to sell their work and sometimes did. The true photographic hobbyist waited in the wings of history, offstage; his time had not yet arrived.

All in their appointed turns brought differing points of view to what they deemed worthy of their efforts. They ranged from the most sophisticated to the most naive and innocent. For some, the impulse to record and celebrate their existence or capture a momentous occurrence overrode their ability to manipulate the heavy and complex equipment of their time. Too often the personality and the demands of their subjects and the situations offered superseded the personality and the outlook of the photographer. In other cases the reverse was true. They were not free

agents as is the contemporary hobbyist, ranging the world in his leisure time to record it with color film and automatic equipment. What is here to see is the full range of interaction between personalities involved in the preserving of history and in the making of history as well. So far as these views present themselves and imply no more, they are faithful to history and thus believable.

Emerging on the following pages of this book, then, are not only the oft-told tales of major glories, accomplishments, and heroism that fill our history books. Preserved here are the common, ordinary characteristics of day-to-day life on the nineteenth-century Western frontier. Suggested in enormous tragic detail is the somberness, the loneliness, the frustrations, the questionings, the hesitations, the petty successes, and the tragedies, great and small that dominated everyday living in many frontier communities.

Plain people can be observed in shabby clothes, in their unpretentious styles, facing the photographer's camera with a sense of their own significance. These men, women, and their children seem understandably unable to display for the photographer the enormous pride and satisfaction we know they felt living in a society, which by comparison with the Old World of their childhoods, seems free and full of opportunities for each of them. They mask the excitement they nurtured, feeding their belief that these infant communities might allow each of them realization of long-cherished dreams.

These pictures can challenge us if we let them. They draw a sobering picture of a time not too long ago when fundamental values were rooted in accomplishment and men could live and die aware and satisfied that some portion of their destiny lay in their own hands. It is this point that dominates all others as I look at these photographs. The men and women pictured here have taken charge of their lives, succeeding and failing. They offer the photographer this confidence, this energy, this forthrightness. They are willing to enter into a combined effort with the photographer to present themselves as they think they are, with no frills and no nonsense at all. This quality, this interaction between the photographers and those working men and women they photographed gives much pointed meaning to lives more clearly understood then than the ones we see around us now shadowed by alienation, fear, suspicion, and hatred.

The chief pleasure for me in these photographs is the affirmation of life the people presented here offer to the reader. These people are good to look upon. They are forthright, sturdy, open-faced in mien and in manner. These are individuals asking to be accepted as humans, not as figures of influence or wealth alone. Their very challenging relationship with the camera is a mighty expression of the democratic instincts Whitman found such joy in celebrating. As an expression of that Whitmanesque enthusiasm then, this book and I salute our nineteenth-century immigrants and the democratic foundations they built.

Opposite page:
Stereoscopic card illustration.
Photographers, Silas & Lewis Melander, Chicago, 1876.

Below:
Buffalo Bill's Wild West Show Indian.
Photographers, Burke & Koretke, Chicago, circa 1900.

1
The American Dream

A powerful component in the immigrant's dream to become an American was the deeply sensed understanding that at its core lay a new type of life, one of option and personal choice. For these immigrants, their legacy from the Old World was a life in which they provided the hands and the muscles and did only what they were told. They tended not to participate in judgments and social choices, realizing in a profound and sad fashion that their own destiny was not theirs to control. As adults this tragic understanding could be borne, but for their children's future it was a deep sense of hopelessness that drove them to find some way of life that would be different. They looked for improvement that could be seen and enjoyed in their own lifetime. It was this stubborn belief that brought them to the United States, moving deeper into the unknown and the unwanted areas, places previously considered too poor or too dangerous for white men. The simple beauty of this picnic in the midst of a cowshed, itself a paraphrase of beauty in the mire, emphasizes some of the beliefs nineteenth-century Americans wished to live by. Here is a latter-day Abraham Lincoln reading by firelight. This young man struggling to make sense out of new words, new letters, new ideas, and new thoughts is almost oblivious of his companion. Such commitment to learning symbolized for him, for her, and for their families the real possibility of becoming a new type of man and woman in this curious new land.

These nineteenth-century Europeans brought with them thousand-year-old skills of every type. They knew the land. In their meager beginnings, the stuff of the land was the source of their homes, their clothing, their food, and their very substance. The materials were not always the most enduring; we would label them primitive in our time. They were wood and grasses, substances forever endangered by natural and man-made disasters: fire, flood, and wind. Such structures were frequently unventilated, cold in the winter, fervid in the summer heat. Nonetheless, their hearths, their fireplaces, their pitiful shabby dwellings initiated belief that their struggle to become Americans, to become new people in a new time, would indeed triumph.

Unidentified children study in a Pennsylvania barn, 1887.
Photographer unknown.

Above:
Farm scene in northeastern United States, circa 1890.
Photographer unknown.

Opposite:
Pennsylvania farm woman weaving homespun cloth, 1883.
Photographer unknown.

Following page:
Hotel in Sandwich, Illinois, circa 1885.
Photographer unknown.

Blacksmith shop,
Sandwich, Illinois, circa 1885.
Photographer unknown.

The old inevitably gave way to the new. Styles and decoration, as well as skills in construction, could be seen in buildings in which two families, or three, or even four might live in concord. These buildings became the fashion of the day in towns growing into villages, in villages changing into cities. For many, it was common to live out one's life tramping board sidewalks and dirt streets, sharing them with admiring citizens. As fortunes for towns and citizens alike changed for the better, so did changing life-styles follow in their wake.

For many of us, to look back on our lives as children and beyond even to the childhood of our parents in this land is to recognize certain experiences largely beyond our ken today. For instance, shopping, that efficient, impersonal operation we know in our time has replaced the former opportunity to wander, look, and smell, to browse, to ponder choices, to spend a few precious pennies in pleasant leisure. We knew then that spending was in and of itself a joy, a type of neighborliness. From our point of view today, it seems quaint to see bird cages, penny candy, leather, coffeepots, and other items abundant in nineteenth-century grocery stores. In those days they were aromatic heavens for children. The stores were a bewildering experience of sight, sound, and color hard to forget. The abundance and variety of wares was a reassurance that their dreams for a better life would come to pass, reassurance they badly needed.

Above:
Mr. Stearns' General Store, circa 1885.
Photographer unknown.

Opposite:
Interior of drygoods store, Sandwich, Illinois, 1885.
Photographer unknown.

Baltimore fire scene.
Photographer unknown.

The rigors of the new life were many, as they would be in any new land. The ancient and dreaded enemy, "fire," was among the foremost. It was not strange that, built largely of wood, few cities on the early frontier escaped major damage more than once. As a result, the settlers quickly organized their own primitive fire departments. They were built and manned with the equipment the townsmen could afford and depended on the combined efforts of those who had to endure the savage consequences of a crippling fire. And after the fires came floods. Rivers and creeks uncontrolled, undammed, fed by melting snows, and heightened by roaring rains, created damage beyond man's ability to conceive. Clearing up after the Johnstown Flood of 1911 is a classic example of the kind of obliterating tragedy the floods could bring.

Opposite:
Johnstown flood, 1889.
Photographer unknown.

Below:
The Boston fire of 1872.
Photographer unknown.

Following page:
Kansas City flood of 1903.
Photographer unknown.

Above:
New Hampshire flour mill, 1874.
Photographer, B. W. Kilburn.

Left:
Textile factory, Connecticut, circa 1885.
Photographer unknown.

To those new Americans coming from the countryside in Europe the growing cities in the New World were a source of wonder. The excitement, the mad rush, the blaze of color, the varied activities made boredom an impossibility. Yet underlying the razzle-dazzle was a form of anonymity, a crushing, nameless lack of recognition. The cities, as they grew, sequestered most of the new arrivals into ghettos, strictly enforcing the segregation on which they fed. Towering structures generated a numbing lack of a sense of identity. Workmen were herded into factories for long hours of work and dreadful wages under poor working conditions. They lived out their tired lives in alienation, often side by side with their working children.

Above:
Market on Beekman Street, New York, 1895.
Photographer unknown.

Opposite page:
New York, New York, circa 1885.
Photographer, Edwin Rew.

Right:
Connecticut textile mill, circa 1890.
Photographer, Silas Melander.

Opposite page:
New Orleans street scene, late 1880s.
Photographer unknown.

Right:
Five Points, Atlanta, Georgia, circa 1880.
Photographer, Silas Melander.

Below:
Richmond, Virginia, late 1880s.
Photographer unknown.

In the growing centers of the East there was tragic identity between the cities and their immigrant victims. Those whom society had cast off were condemned to live in those portions of the city that were similarly rejected—the meanest, the lowest, the most difficult. These were the areas one might likely find the new arrivals, bewildered humans struggling to find a place in the new order. The history of black people in the United States is all too consonant with the oldest, most decrepit quarters and, as a rule, the meanest jobs. It is hard to find adequate graphic records of the struggle these black people waged for a meaningful life in the United States. The burden for the dispossessed in the great cities was anonymity and alienation. These photographs offer us a bare glimpse of people living out their lives in the ignominy of city-jungles, pitiful monuments to a vain struggle for equal opportunity as Americans.

Canal Street, New Orleans,
Louisiana, late 1880s.
Photographer unknown.

Fort Worth, Texas, street scene, circa 1888.
Photographer unknown.

Los Angeles, California, circa 1900.
Photographer unknown.

Portland, Oregon, circa 1885.
Photographer unknown.

PORTLAND SEED CO.

SEEDS
Poultry Supplies
Flour & Feed

THE FAVORITE BOAT HOUSE
LAUNCHES & ROW BOATS
FOR RENT

LAUNCHES TO THE FAIR

Above:
South Water Street, Chicago, circa 1889.
Photographer unknown.

Right:
South Water Market, Chicago, 1873.
Photographers, Copelin and Melander.

Traffic jams are not the unique contribution of the automobile. It was images of Chicago such as we see here that compelled Carl Sandburg to express awe and admiration for the restless, growing Midwest empire. Patient teamsters, enduring men, thread a path for their teams through clogged streets. A struggle for economic survival blusters about them, emphasizing the brutal vigor required to live and work in the great city-jungles. Massive commercial empires rested on the never-ending, round-the-clock labor of city dwellers toiling in obscurity and loneliness—a price for their dreams most immigrants did not realize.

31

Chicago street scene, 1873.
Photographers, Copelin and Melander.

For those who came first to Chicago, when that great midwestern city was the economic empire of the West, it was easier to understand the transformation of the frontier into the new cities. There was little to see in Chicago that looked different from what was evident and similar in Philadelphia, Boston, and New York. The window dressing of the new technology was here in abundance: telephone wires, rails for streetcars, paved streets and sidewalks, street lamps, modern stores, and towering buildings of awesome size. In all respects, the configuration, the feel, the smell, the look was of the East, and yet, this Chicago, this commercial hub, this transport center, was the doorway to the growing Far West and the center of what was then regarded as the West. Immigrants left Chicago to meet the plains, the mountains, and finally, the Pacific slope, there to establish in everyone's mind the full nature and known location of the whole American West.

Waterfront at Leavenworth, Kansas, 1867.
Photographer, E. E. Henry.

The vital arteries for national expansion were the rails and the rivers. Often the rails were flung independent of one another across this immense land. National need and competition for gain were most often in conflict, and ordered growth was unusual. There were points on the land where rail and river met, doing so with enormous satisfaction to those who desperately counted on them for good fortune. Such couplings resulted in cities, towns, and villages, and frequently in nothing more distinguished than landings. Leavenworth Landing is an example of the mechanical and commercial efficiency of such twinings, demonstrating the new industrial beauty they produced upon the land.

Above:
The steamboat *Silver Bow* making for Leavenworth Landing in 1867.
Picture taken from the south esplanade.
Photographer, E. E. Henry.

Mark Twain pointed out that there is an air about rivers, a quality in the light that surrounds a river. Serenity shades a river, and the hot sun dapples the still water with the aid of an old tree's leaves. There is joy in the beauty of the graceful steamboats man has constructed to move upon the river, and the Missouri River, in our photographer's time, combined all of these pleasures. One could feel release in walking along the banks of a busy river. It was an endless, moving spectacle of sound, sight, and color. To have seen the growing West under such conditions was to have seen sights never to be duplicated. It was not possible to duplicate them, and the photographs accurately catch the sense of what was commonplace and soul catching in Leavenworth over a hundred years ago.

Close-up of the Missouri riverboat *Silver Bow,* docked at
Leavenworth Landing, 1867.
Photographer, E. E. Henry.

Above:
Leavenworth railroad depot, 1867.
Photographer, E. E. Henry.

Railroad travel was not always the plush convenience that most of us living today can recall. In an earlier time it was still a convenience, albeit a discomforting one. Straight-backed wooden seats were not velvet-covered; they were not upholstered at all. There were no windows in the early cars, only window openings. The cinders and oily smoke were free for the passengers, asked for or not. In addition to the hard seats, there were no dining cars to help make a long journey a pleasure. The stops were often and long, and the stations offered few comforts to ease the tedium of the slow, old, coal-burning engines. These immigrants arrived under conditions they considered relative luxury. Newer cars with rooftop ventilators to provide fresh air were their good fortune —an uncalled for blessing. These crude vehicles were chariots of opportunity for new immigrants. They brought them to the prairies full of hope and passion, determined to build a new life on the western frontier.

Opposite:
Passengers arriving on a train in Leavenworth, Kansas, 1867.
Photographer, E. E. Henry.

Shawnee Street, Leavenworth, Kansas, 1869.
Photographer, E. E. Henry.

New arrivals found the new towns contradictory
and surprising. They were built on the floors of the
prairies; the very streets were the earth of the prairie.
From wooden, planked walks, the town's main street
revealed a full horizon of commercial opportunity.
There were few businesses, housed in everything from

wood shanties to fairly opulent brick buildings, that did not shout their commodities and their services to the new settlers. It sometimes appeared that the main street was simply a huge advertisement for the ubiquitous talents of sign-painters. In every case the boardwalks were shaded from the sun that gave equally of its searing heat to man and beast. This same life-giving orb helped create products and crops that transformed this dusty wilderness into a food basket for the United States; and for certain products, it was the food basket for the world. There was no end of interest in these struggling little prairie towns.

Above:
Leavenworth, Kansas, 1869.
Photographer, E. E. Henry.

Opposite:
Leavenworth, 1869.
Photographer, E. E. Henry.

There was more in a prairie town's streets than merely business signs and merchants. It was a center for investment. Construction was everywhere; open areas of land were quickly snapped up for investment. Real estate and banking flourished because they were desperately needed. In these towns, frantic commercial efforts reproduced in a small way the look of teeming eastern metropolises. It is a curious contradiction that those who left the great cities of the East for the relative freedom and potential for individuality of the West struggled with all their might to create in new prairie locations the very commercial prisons they had originally left with great joy and relief.

Following page:
Delaware Street, Leavenworth, 1869.
Photographer, E. E. Henry.

43

Naivete stood cheek by jowl with flamboyant boosterism in the new prairie cities. Here, for example, next to a newly installed gas streetlight are two undistinguished lumps of coal on public display. They are a proud civic monument, a gesture of self-esteem to the determination of a citizenry endlessly defeated in their search for needed coal. Miners pursued the search tirelessly; drilling just another fifty feet brought success and with it a new role for the valued coal as public sculpture. It is astonishing to find the rapidity

with which eastern refinements were brought to prairie frontier metropolises—for example, steam printing, the application of power to the centuries-old, hand-fed printing press. Here on this main street the photograph reveals a steam printing shop ready to play its indispensable role as transforming agent. In their ability to communicate rapidly and widely, printing presses were a major unifying force linking the western frontier to the eastern centers.

Opposite page and above:
First National Bank of Leavenworth,
early 1860s.
Photographer, Ralph Stevenson.

There were those commercial institutions built with such foresight, care, and consideration for the future that they have structurally endured as commercial institutions of solid worth. Such is the First National Bank of Leavenworth, Kansas. Who cannot admire the delicately, near-Georgian grace and charm of this building that stands in some isolation on one of the major street corners of this important western city?

Below:
Circus parade passing in front of the First National Bank
Building of Leavenworth, Kansas, circa 1880.
Photographer, Harrison Putney.

Imperial pride lived in America. Our national symbol, the rampant eagle, seized the hearts of those who knew it with distaste as a national symbol of some of the countries from which they had come in the Old World. Carved, gilded, poised for flight, and erected, if possible, to tower over everything else in the city, the eagle was a glorious example of American determination to soar higher and higher, supreme over everything. Such ornaments provided the sense of aspiration and determination that so marked the citizenry of many frontier cities. It is fitting and proper to find this monstrous eagle suspending from its beak a clock, the eternal recorder of vanishing time. Among the valuable ingredients that Americans .treasured was time: time to be used, time to be spent, time to be invested profitably. It was a combination of endless determination and time spent profitably that marked the spirit of those who built the cities of the prairie.

49

Looking west up Fifth Street, Leavenworth, Kansas, 1869.
Photographer, E. E. Henry.

At first glance, Fifth Street (Leavenworth, Kansas, 1869) may seem almost indistinguishable from the streets of a hundred other towns. But closer examination (note marked areas on the contact print and blowups of those areas) gives us a rare personal view of Leavenworth. These enlargements of minute areas of the glass plate negative provide a true picture of the details that made Leavenworth unique. From a travel announcement of a steamboat tour to the solemnity of the now classic cigar store Indian—Leavenworth offered a wide variety of experiences and services for its inhabitants and for those who flocked to the town in the 1870s.

TOBACCO.

PHEL

CHA'S FEESS.

DEALER IN

CIGARS

AND

TOBACCO

J. SAMUEL

MERCHANT TAILOR

CUTTING CLEANING

&

REPAIRING

DONE TO ORDER

DWIFE

SO A WATER.

BLU LICK WATER.

Mr. Robert Parham's Drug Store on Cherokee Street, Leavenworth, Kansas, 1869.
Photographer, E. E. Henry.

As the prairie cities grew, their spectacle on the wide plains became more and more impressive to their inhabitants and to visitors alike. The once-struggling riverside hamlet of Leavenworth, Kansas, became a major community, a budding city, and in time, a center of importance in the burgeoning Middle West. This panorama showing a profusion of streets, houses, public and commercial buildings, colleges, and farms explains the transformation of the once quiet Kansas plains into a major commercial center. It was an inspiration for those determined to expand the city even farther, as well as for those who saw Leavenworth as a center for their movement farther West. Most significantly, it was a model of what could be built by men and women pursuing the dreams that brought them to America, the hopeful land.

Panoramic view of Leavenworth, Kansas, 1869.
Photographer, E. E. Henry.

People of Leavenworth.
Photographs taken 1860s to 1890s.

56

Portraits of Leavenworth people
from the 1860s to the early 1900s.
*Photographers, E. E. Henry, Harrison Putney,
Ralph Stevenson, and Horace Stevenson.*

Mr. Holm's perpetual motion machine,
Leavenworth, Kansas, circa 1890.
Photographer, Horace Stevenson.

By the turn of the nineteenth century the time for wars against mythological beasts and superhuman enemies had passed in midwestern America. Our heroes then, our sagas and epics, were built around men and women of commerce and intellect. The images of the time reflect these new passions. It is fitting that we can show this paternal photograph of many young employees of the Lemp Beer Company gathered in concert to express their unity, their pleasure for their new life, and their determination to build bigger and bigger commercial success.

There were in abundance then many men and women who struggled to solve the problem of perpetual motion. Although the strange devices they built were unfailingly unsuccessful, they were in most cases ingenious, exciting, and challenging. They were at the same time a source of painful ridicule for their builders. Their devices remained a monument to inventiveness and to the determination to succeed at all costs, a spirit that is still in good health in the United States.

Below:
Unknown Leavenworth family,
picture taken in 1869.
Photographer, E. E. Henry.

Opposite:
Family scene taken
in Leavenworth, Kansas, 1869.
Photographer, E. E. Henry.

Industry and inventiveness produced their own rewards for some, not for all. For those who succeeded and became town leaders there could be a life of near-Victorian opulence to be enjoyed. This new luxury marked the Middle West. The family as the center of a satisfying world, strong in unity, solid in paternal tyranny, became the hallmark of the new community leader. Well-dressed families, well outfitted, posing in classically accepted symbols of family pleasure were the popular image of success. This desired image became a specialty of photographers of the period. These views of connubial bliss, of family warmth, of the kind of success one looked for, were acknowledged with pride in the Middle West. Perhaps they help explain the deep conservatism with which life was approached on this new frontier.

Pages 64–65:
Hauling the new flag pole through Leavenworth,
Kansas, circa 1880.
Photographer, Harrison Putney.

On another scale, there were success symbols of a different kind. The ability to replace the use of brute force in manipulating nature by the effectiveness of the emerging technologies became the hallmark of the managers, the foremen, and the engineers. For the foreigner, the immigrants, and the new arrivals among the workmen, the age-old skills of brawn and simple tools were still demanded. There was no problem, however bizarre, that could not be manipulated successfully, as the tracking of this eighty-foot, wooden beam down the center of a busy city street somewhere in the American West so clearly illustrates.

Colonel W. H. Whetmore of Fort Leavenworth, Kansas, 1869. *Photographer, E. E. Henry.*

Opposite:
Soldiers in front of Fort Leavenworth barracks, 1869. *Photographer, E. E. Henry.*

To furnish the protection and the security demanded by the new settlers required the army to maintain major military posts like this one, Fort Leavenworth. Ancient in its structures, it was up-to-date in its practices and enjoyed the respect of anyone looking to it for assistance and comfort. It housed officers and units of renown, men whose names would become household gossip in a nation girding for what we called our "Indian Wars." Uniform regulations, in this, the postwar, peacetime army were much relaxed, and it was possible to find curious combinations of the military and the civilian in the dress of some soldiers.

As was true in most circumstances of frontier growth, Fort Leavenworth reflected the old and the new in its buildings and equipment. The comfort of the common soldiers was of the least concern to military brass, and the ordinary barracks here were antiquated beyond belief—even for that time. They offered little in the way of pleasure or comfort for those souls who were required to live in them or those trying to think of them as a "home away from home." Massive and strong, they did loom on the post grounds as impressive monuments to martial splendor.

Seventh Cavalry soldiers' barracks,
Leavenworth, Kansas, 1869.
Photographer, E. E. Henry.

The post featured several distinguished resi-
dences for their time, wooden structures that housed
field grade and general officers only. This particular
dwelling, the Syracuse House, was for a brief period
the home of the well-known, vainglorious warrior
George Armstrong Custer. Resplendent in full military dress, imperious in his arrogance, the same
belligerent disdain that characterized much of his
command and caused his tragic death at the Little Big
Horn in 1876, are evident even in this idyllic setting

The Civil War was over when these photographs were taken. The peacetime army's role on the frontier was not clearly defined; its national prestige was far less important than it was in the wartime years. The soldiers in *this* army were different, in themselves an interesting study. One could find curious combinations of the old and the young, the shaven and the bearded, the fit and the unfit in this postwar army on the frontier. Men who had enjoyed command during the war became soldiers without commands and found their places in new relationships. The army included not only the firm, the well, and the determined, those able to serve effectively but the sick and the ailing as well. In this appealing photograph we are witness to a time-less example of the comforting camaraderie existing between humans in difficulty. Here are the healthy creating opportunities to bring comfort and pleasure to those confined to their beds in cheerless hospital wards.

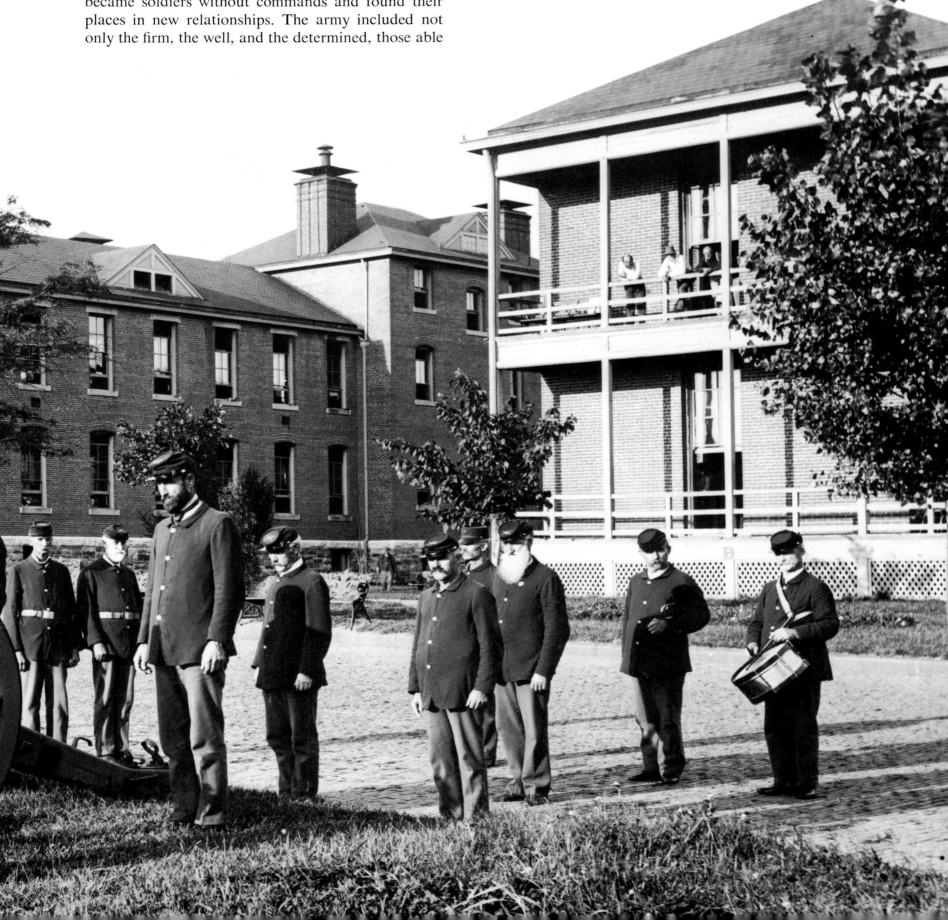

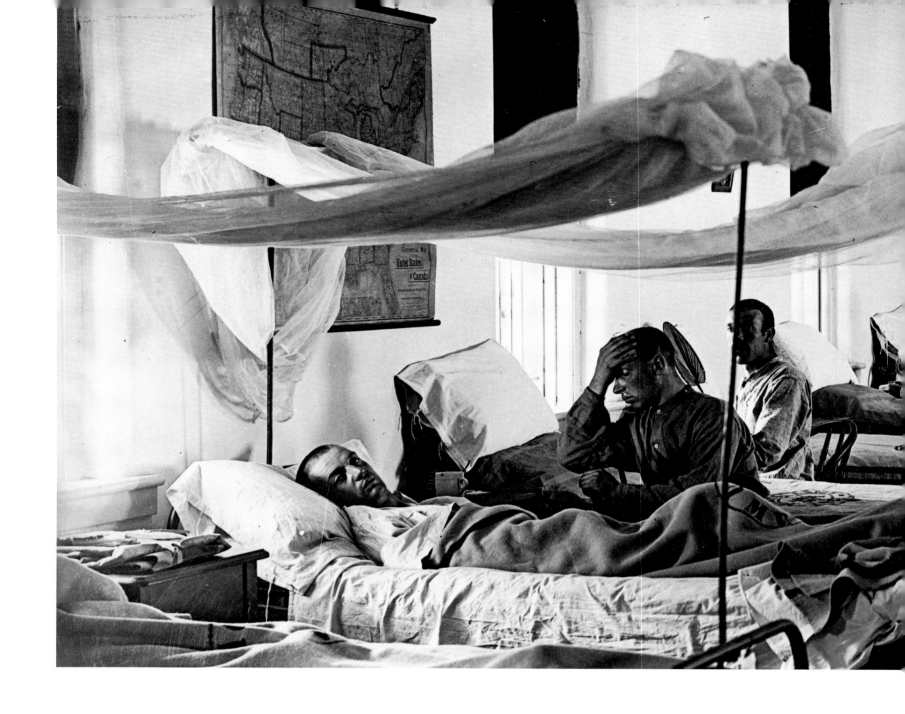

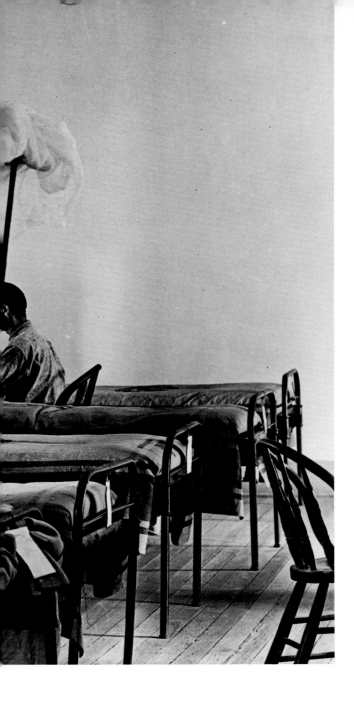

Interior views of Fort Leavenworth
Post Hospital, 1875.
Photographer, E. E. Henry.

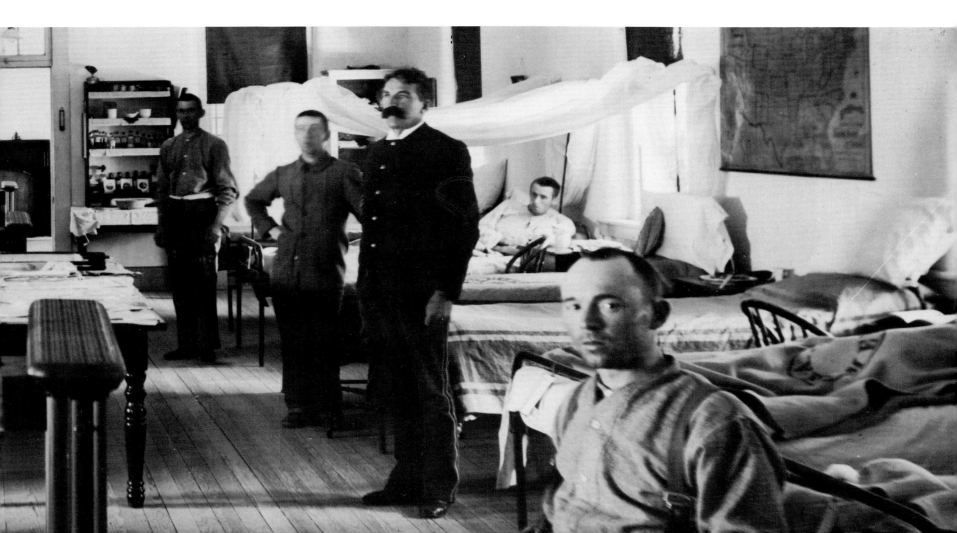

There were always some transgressors. It proved impossible to organize large numbers of human beings in social relationships and not find some transgressors. Here in preparation for their confinements in the post jail, Lansing Prison, we find army prisoners undergo-ing the barbering required by the military regulations. This uniformity helped transform each prisoner into a common animal, easily identified, easily observed, easily organized, easily administered, and effectively kept under the ordered conditions of confinement.

Army veterans at Wadsworth Military Retirement Home, circa 1885.
Photographer, E. E. Henry.

South of Leavenworth there was the Wadsworth home for disabled, volunteer soldiers. It offered old soldiers the opportunity to get together and relive old campaigns and old glories. Those who had retired from the military life gathered at the home to remember their youth, drink beer, see old comrades with pleasure, count the living, and remember the dead. Mainly they lied to one another with the affectionate recognition that their stories were the necessary meat and drink for those who endured into old age.

2
The Way West

California-bound freight wagon, circa 1880.
Photographer unknown.

For some immigrants there was no end to travel, for there was always a little farther to go. Forever there remained an expanding frontier, new opportunity, and new options. Another day brought a new chance to clothe yesterday's dream in new dress, and there was nothing that moved that was not used to transform the itching foot into the wanderer. Most common were the many variations of the canvas-covered wagon, overloaded with freight, ambition, and hopes, drawn by horses, oxen, or whatever beast could pull most effectively. The trail always led over the almost indistinguishable roads leading into the western wilderness.

Below:
Freight wagons on the Santa Fe Trail, circa 1880.
Photographer unknown.

These transcontinental wanderers journeyed through heat and dust, through areas that were known and unknown. They endured misdirection, poor direction, and no direction. They arrived often at hotels that were merely the shabbiest board buildings without heat, without beds, and utterly lacking in even primitive facilities for comfort. They came over the mountains in the summer, and in the bitter winters, they plowed through snow depths so deep as to require crews of men to clear the tracks of the new railways. Almost nothing seemed to stand in the way of the determination and ingenuity of these men, women, and their wandering families to move west a few more miles.

Right:
The Bear Gulch Hotel near Yellowstone Park, circa 1885.
Photographer unknown.

Below:
High in the Colorado mountains both passengers and crew
work to dig a train out of the snow, circa 1880.
Photographer unknown.

Opposite page, above:
Miners' Camp near Socorro, New Mexico, 1882.
Photographer, Joseph E. Smith.

Below:
Group portrait, Socorro, New Mexico, 1882.
Photographer, Joseph E. Smith.

Opposite page, below:
Bringing supplies to miner's camp, Kelly, New Mexico, 1884.
Photographer, Joseph E. Smith.

For these travelers there could be no such thing as defeat. Whatever could move or could be repaired to move was pressed into service to move families and goods westward. The endless migration was witness to many pitiful sights. Careworn, mud-stained, chafed and warped by wind, rain, snow, and fierce heat, conveyances such as the ones seen in these photos made their slow way across the wide plains and snowy mountains. They were driven by men and women, and boys and girls when they were required, all of leathery countenances, fully prepared to move yet another day. They were learning to live off the land, eating food they had never known before, sometimes infrequently. These photographs express some of the deep pride with which they regarded their hard-won accomplishments. They sum up their satisfying beliefs that they were living the American dream successfully, that their personal shining future was "out there" somewhere.

Left:
Captain Jack Crawford,
U.S. Cavalry Scout,
Socorro, New Mexico, 1883.
Photographer, Joseph E. Smith.

Our immigrants and our native born were not all wise, noble, and God-fearing. One could find every evidence of vanity, ambition, success, and failure among them. Look at the dandy on the left. He is garbed as a plainsman, leaning on his rifle as no plainsman would ever dare, with a pistol stuck in his belt in the best position to shoot the wooden leg he stands upon. We are actually seeing a poet posing for his admirers back home—an erstwhile poet determined to pass himself off as the poet of the plains. Facing away from him in arrogant obscurity on the opposite page is Joe Fowler. His efforts to live long failed; after unhappily dangling at the end of a strong rope, he wound up in an unmarked grave in an unknown town "out there." His mortal remains became in time part of the rich soil western farmers depended upon for the West's amazing fertility. Ah! poor, poor Joe Fowler.

87

They lived, these hardy people, as they were required to live by circumstances—and no more. Whatever aspirations they brought with them for eventual luxury were deeply hidden against the immeasurable demands of the land they crossed and settled upon. The prospector literally lived on the land, not knowing his next stopping place, not knowing the sources of his pitiful pleasures. He looked endlessly for water and gold and in that precise and life-saving order, always.

Those who stopped in a hopeful location built with what the area afforded. It was common enough to find sod shanties, in which both peat and buffalo chips were used for fuel. Where wood was available, cabins of the most primitive character were built. We see here several examples of the kind of temporary dwellings, the truest examples of the shacks and shanties the settler called "home."

Opposite page:
Family in front of their Nebraska
sod house, circa 1880.
Photographer unknown.

Right:
Arizona prospector, circa 1883.
Photographer unknown.

Below:
Colorado family, circa 1890.
Photographer unknown.

In New Mexico, where the rigors of uncertain weather, summer or winter, could be less severe than many other locations, it was possible to build combinations of homes and businesses that were effective, sometimes bizarre, and forever interesting. This sagging saloon and billiard emporium above, built of adobe brick and wood salvaged from packing crates, stands ready, with its portly one-armed bartender in attendance, to dispense Wm. J. Lemp's St. Louis Lager Beer to all who might come to Kelly, New Mexico—day or night. For the more sober minded, S. B. Chapin, M.D., dispensed drugs for the weary, the broken, and the alcoholically ineffective, as well as paints, oils, brushes, cigars, stationery, choice perfumes, lamps, and fine soaps for the discriminating.

Above:
Billiard hall and saloon near Kelly, New Mexico, 1883.
Photographer, Joseph E. Smith.

Right:
Dr. Chapin's Office and Drug Store near Kelly,
New Mexico, 1882.
Photographer, Joseph E. Smith.

Kelly, New Mexico, 1883.
Photographer, Joseph E. Smith.

As an unknown Irishman named Murphy lent his name to a gold-mining camp in California in 1849, so did another unknown Irish migrant donate his to the up-and-coming community of Kelly, New Mexico. Kelly's main street is typical of many small town main streets in the American West. A dusty plain lined on both sides with board sidewalks and temporary wooden buildings, its ubiquitous signs flaunt the commodities of earnest merchants hoping to find quick fortunes. This kind of main street with its wooden facade has been most popular with movie producers. Everything happened here except the face-to-face shootouts, the ambushes, the many childish myths that have transformed the hard-working West into an unbelievable orgy of sex, gunplay, card sharks, honest and venal sheriffs, and endless violence.

A large part of the truth of the workaday West lay in the endless, back-breaking monotonous work required to transform a hot, dusty plain as in Socorro, New Mexico, into a thriving city of buildings—wooden, brick, and adobe. In Socorro, the ancient and the new coexist side by side. These Mexican workmen are molding adobe clay into bricks, stacking them to dry in the hot sun, using methods and tools as old as the first men of any color to come into the Southwest. To meet the scourge of fire, the Socorrans finally learned to build well with combinations of area fieldstone and red brick. It demonstrated their skill and their good taste, as can be seen in this strongly built warehouse and stage station.

Socorro, New Mexico, 1882.
Photographer, Joseph E. Smith.

Making adobe bricks,
Socorro, New Mexico,
1882.
*Photographer,
Joseph E. Smith.*

Barber shop, Denver, Colorado, circa 1885.
Photographer unknown.

And in Denver, Colorado, to the east and high in the Rocky Mountains, civilization developed to the point where, in elegant brick buildings, men could have their hair cut, take a bath, and listen to canaries at the same time. It is not clear whether these splendid specimens posing for their photograph have, or intend to.

Opposite page:
Cowboys spear the brass ring, Socorro, New Mexico, 1882.
Photographer, Joseph E. Smith.

Immediately below:
Bronco-busting, Socorro, New Mexico, 1884.
Photographer, Joseph E. Smith.

Not everyone came to the land to build upon it. There were those, and in the beginning there were many, who saw the land as an area in which cattle might be raised successfully. These ranchers needed only the land, forage, and more than anything else—water. And here we see examples of the kinds of spreads, in the middle of nowhere, that were character-istic of the cattle industry throughout the West and, in this case, New Mexico. They were doomed in the march of time, because inevitably the land proved too valuable to be used only for roaming cows to be sold and slaughtered once. Such spreads were later replaced by cities.

Cattle grazing near Socorro, New Mexico, 1883.
Photographer, Joseph E. Smith.

Idaho Springs, 1874.
Photographer, B. W. Kilburn.

This view of Idaho Springs, Idaho, is the antithesis of the ranch. Here is an example of an orderly planned city, quietly anticipating its future growth, surrounding itself and building within it all of the ingredients for a commercial population: homes, businesses, churches, and roads. Within the vista of all, at that point, lies a trackless West, one potentially exciting, for investment, for growth, and for development. This, in many ways, is the archetype of the dream that the immigrants brought with them to this curious, strange land.

Socorro, New Mexico, 1882.
Photographer, Joseph E. Smith.

Socorro, New Mexico, 1882.
Photographer, Joseph E. Smith.

Saloon in Socorro, New Mexico, 1882.
Photographer, Joseph E. Smith.

Our immigrants came with deep prides and deep satisfactions to be met. Frequently the names of their buildings expressed their enormous pleasure in their own accomplishments. There is something naively exciting about naming a saloon "Our Office." It is dubious that this reflected the satisfaction of all of this town's citizens, but clearly it did for many. The portrait photographer of the time became the enshriner of the ambitions, the secret desires, the satis-

factions, and the fantasies of the citizens, both permanent and transient. Witness, on one hand, the standstill in the faked duel between cardplayers and whiskey drinkers, all young, all cigar-smoking, all unbearded, and all naive. Perhaps the two almost sinister women somberly, interestingly draped and kneeling, smoking their cigarettes, portended the women's liberation movement of today.

Recognizing well the imperatives of communication, information, and opinion, as well as the community-organizing character of newspapers, few Western cities failed to solicit and attract the roving job printer. Most printers correctly sensed in the growing communities opportunities for a stable and influential future. Photographed in natural light this primitive, frontier printshop lets us see a pressman at the stone in the foreground, a typesetter distributing hand types at the left, and an elderly, bearded pressman, almost intellectual in appearance, feeding handbills into the little "clamshell" printing press. The

Mark Twain-appearing gentleman, with cravat, standing in supervisory capacity is most likely the editor remembering his ever-present responsibility to tap the conscience of the town and speak its mind.

Printshop in Socorro, New Mexico, 1882.
Photographer, Joseph E. Smith.

Pottery shop, Socorro, New Mexico, 1882.
Photographer, Joseph E. Smith.

106

It must not be thought that art did not flourish on the frontier. The process of coming to the West was not only a coarsening one; it coexisted with a persistent struggle to maintain sensitivity to beauty, a feeling for form and color, and a love of grace and elegance. Deeply inherited from centuries of such traditions in the Old Country, aesthetic feelings and perceptions survived and thrived on the frontier. Few towns of immigrants failed to produce furniture, pottery, artifacts, and homes that were not only utilitarian but were at the same time examples of great beauty and grace. These common enough pots and jugs being produced by a local potter exhibit a warm sensitivity to handsomeness in form. It is good to believe that the townspeople who purchased them were warmed as well by their innate loveliness.

Overriding all other activities on the frontier was industry. The ability to attract industry, large scale industry if possible, was the opportunity most eagerly looked for by every town leader. Townspeople even invested in spurious schemes in the frantic belief that such con games would bring the railroad to their town and make it into a major shipping center. This town has found the railroad or, maybe, the railroad found it. Whatever the reason, this fortunate town is busy repairing locomotives using the overhead, belt-driven machinery of the period. This was a time of make-do and dark, gloomy workshops—the breeding ground for a generation of Yankee mechanics. Companion to such workmen were those citizens who, recognizing the danger of fire from increased industrial activity, created a local fire fighting department. Their pride in the new fire bell, the hand-pulled hose cart, and the bright red uniforms is all pardonable when the brutal, exhausting work they performed is considered.

Opposite:
Repairing locomotive steam engine,
Socorro, New Mexico, 1886.
Photographer, Joseph E. Smith.

Below:
Socorro Fire Department, circa 1885.
Photographer, Joseph E. Smith.

There was the play of every kind then, not as much as we know today, certainly not in as many forms, and certainly not the kind of play that was brought by television screens to passive observers. It was participatory play, and here is an example of the way the young played.

Below:
Boys having a boxing match in the streets of Socorro,
New Mexico, circa 1882.
Photographer, Joseph E. Smith.

Following page:
Quarter horse racing in the streets of Socorro,
New Mexico, 1884.
Photographer, Joseph E. Smith.

Not to be outdone, and perhaps on the same days as their sons and daughters, their fathers played, and their play took the form of rough competition of all kinds. These were contests, watermelon eating contests, pie eating contests, races of all kinds, and most exciting was the combination of man and beast. Here is a headlong dash of hatless men racing for the honor of riding the fastest horse along dusty town streets, stirred by jubilant and frantic audiences cheering their particular contestant on to victory.

Socorro grocery store scene, 1882.
Photographer, Joseph E. Smith.

For the elderly, those resting from a lifetime of shocking labor, there was play that consisted of reminiscence and ease around a warm stove on a cold night. These old men became, in time, revered and honored old-timers. In them were housed the much-loved collection of tales, experiences, hopes, beliefs, truths, and tall tales the whole town lived by. *They* knew what had gone before, *they* were the tellers of ancient history, and *they* were treated with a special respect and a kind of tolerant amusement, as well. Although their lives were drawing to a close, they had earned a secure and honored place in the town's affections. To the end of their days they served a necessary and useful function in these growing towns.

Above:
Socorro, New Mexico, 1882.
Photographer, Joseph E. Smith.

Right:
Socorro, New Mexico, 1882.
Photographer, Joseph E. Smith.

Joseph E. Smith, the photographer, at home with his family at Socorro, New Mexico, circa 1885.

There was, of course, gentility and tenderness; all was not rough horseplay. The need to build stable home lives was strong among the immigrants and was respected. The town photographer, Joseph Smith, created in his own home a scene most characteristic of family life in his time. It was based on self-produced entertainment, utterly dependent on the combined efforts and skills of the whole family. It was expected that gentlewomen might learn to play the piano if it could be afforded, and sing in good voice. Children were taught the songs and were encouraged to join in the family "sing." Family singing was widely recognized as one of the more meaningful rewards to be found in a life lived honestly and well.

Socorro, New Mexico, 1882.
Photographer, Joseph E. Smith.

To counterbalance the joy of life there was always the pain of death. As we today have learned only to *acknowledge* death, they likewise, in their time found it hard to accept. It was always a tragedy. It was ever a loss, and to lose the young, the yet unfullfiled with the promise of tomorrow's good fortune, was a special blow. It was a tragedy more difficult to bear than the expected death of those who had lived out their lives. Perhaps for our tastes now, the affection, the love, the regard with which this photograph of a dead child has been taken seems unpleasant. It is for us to try to understand the special loneliness these people endured, the special sense of loss they felt. The death of their young represented a crushing loss. Their child had not yet had the chance to redeem the sacrifices of his parents or claim the legacy of the promise of his life in this new land.

Golden Alaska

Alaska! Golden Alaska was, in fact, a forested wilderness wetted by melting snows. It was a place cut in every direction by wide rivers, rapids, gorges, and dangerous cataracts. To come to Alaska was to approach it from the Pacific Ocean, from which every path into the interior was a watery one. The way in was the way of the steamboat. Next in popularity were sailing boats and rafts, whatever would float on the many wet trails of this strange, rich, gold-bearing territory.

Alaskan steamboat landing, circa 1897.
Photographer unknown.

Following page:
Enlargement of the Alaskan steamboat landing.

121

The casual, seemingly unorganized activity at most Alaskan steamboat landings was deceptive to the "tenderfoot" newcomer. Although normally familiar at home, it was more bewildering here in the Territory. The steamers seemed forever busy, apparently aimlessly loading and discharging men and goods. The temporary character of the towns, homes, and businesses, and the dislocated relationship of men to their chosen activity all lent confirmation to the strangeness of this new environment. Days and nights were filled with the hoarse shouts and cries of men and beasts struggling to bring order and direction out of mounting chaos. These photographs help introduce us to gold-rush Alaska, as surely the same steamboat landings introduced it to the men and women arriving here to find quick fortunes.

Dawson City, Alaskan gold rush, 1898.
Photographer unknown.

The more notorious of the towns and villages of the Alaskan gold rush live on in legend. Famed Dawson lives in memory in an aura of grandeur unmatched by the reality of these pictures of a somber, tented wilderness. Bordered by a swift-flowing river and shadowed by brooding hills, the town rose to its daily challenges in the classic fashion. Chopping, slashing, burning, clearing—ancient means for new growth were Dawson's answer to the clamoring "cheechakos." The town expanded for utility's need, not beauty, and if it all proved profitable, "That's what we came for, isn't it, boys?"

Dawson City, Alaskan gold rush, 1898.
Photographer unknown.

125

Dawson City, Alaskan gold rush, 1898.
Photographer unknown.

As the river towns grew, they moved from the river flats onto the high ground benches. Then up they crept, slowly, up the shallow slopes of the surrounding hills. Cotton tents were replaced by wooden shacks as quickly as wood for construction was available. Log cabins constructed of unbarked trees, chinked with moss had to suffice, as they had for many of the miners' forefathers. It was rare that a house built of sawn lumber from sawmills in the States could be afforded then, and these few added a needed touch of frontier elegance in these icebox outposts. Anything and everything that would support the *temporary* stay of the miners was pressed into service. "Find gold!" was the eternal cry. A fine point, grasped by only a shrewd few in Dawson was, "Make gold!" Make it by selling supplies, at outrageous prices to anyone who yearned to go out on the frozen trails and find gold.

Dawson City, the Klondyke, 1898.
Photographer unknown.

Makeshift river town during the Alaskan gold rush, 1898.
Photographer unknown.

Bonanza Creek, a tributary of the Yukon River, 1897.
Photographer unknown.

For those who tried to see it, a somber and strange beauty was apparent day and night. There were vivid groupings of bare rock, green trees, rolling hills, and fast-flowing rivers. The counterpoint was man. His excitement, his dispensed energy, the smoke and flame of his campfires, all were evidence of those attempting to live and work in this wild, inhospitable area. They created color and drama in abundance.

River landings, like the one in the photograph, became mirrors for flaming skies at morn and at twilight. The heart-stopping cries of wild animals lent just the pinch of danger man could accept in his efforts to challenge nature. Cloud-filled skies and prolonged rain transformed the wilderness into fogbound dreamlands— *only* for those who tried to see it that way.

131

Turbulent waters of the Yukon River, 1898.
Photographer unknown.

Flat-bottom boat on the
sandbar-ravaged Yukon River, 1897.
Photographer unknown.

The journey by water never ended. From the deep sea to the coast of Alaska the miner's way was up the large rivers to the small rivers, through the gorges, the chasms, the rapids, the small tributaries, using anything that floated: raft, barge, flatboat, bateau, sailing punt, or steamboat. Every craft that could be manipulated and sometimes, those that could not, vessels that were prey to every hidden rock, every submerged reef, every swirling rapid, every change in current were used until they were destroyed by the Alaskan wilderness. This was the *only* way for the thousands of tons of supplies and the thousands of men who believed that the new Eldorado was snow-covered, frozen, and named Alaska.

Crude wooden raft traveling along the Yukon River, 1897. *Photographer unknown.*

Shooting the rapids of the Yukon River, 1897. *Photographer unknown.*

133

The contradiction in gold-rush Alaska was that no place was home and every place was home. The place to stop was where a stop was needed. Small communities struggling to survive were everywhere—by the frozen forests in the winter and along the muddy trails in the summertime. The living competed with the dead as whole communities survived, and others were abandoned. Every place one found was a brutal tribute to the frantic, avid inexperience of those who came to Alaska to find gold.

Miners making camp before ascending Chilkoot Pass, 1897.
Photographer unknown.

135

Steamboat landing that serviced miners of the Alaskan
gold rush, 1898.
Photographer unknown.

Waiting in silent majesty were the steamers, the stern-wheelers. Named in caprice by their builders or their owners—listen to a few names, *Australian, Columbian, Leah, Fanny, Nome City*—they performed dependably. Shallow-draft vessels, highly built, always overloaded, were ever ready, with steam up, to take miners in and gold out. This was the way, this was the trade, and the photographer could find such a photograph to recall their glory.

Mining camp near Chilkoot Pass, 1898.
Photographer unknown.

Following page:
Miners purchasing supplies at the base of Chilkoot Pass, 1898.
Photographer unknown.

Because it was the most easily transportable, the cheapest, the lightest, the most easily dispensed with, and could serve other purposes, the canvas tent was home for the Alaskan goldminer. Tents dotted the landscape and were almost indistinguishable from the patches of winter snow fading in the summer heat. They were a major symbol of the Alaskan gold rush, almost as much as the Conestoga wagon was for those who came to mine gold in California in 1849.

Dominating all else were the miners, the human quotient. They were, in the main, men of vast inexperience, unused to the rigors of gold recovery. They were men for whom snow and ice were a new experience. They were men of every nationality, every language, every size, and every shape. They included honest men, fair men, greedy men, thieves, and rascals. They came to Alaska inadequately clothed and illogically and badly supplied. They came to share one another's experience, to steal it if they could, to make their own fortunes and then, get out and go back home rich men. They knew little of what their fortunes might consist; they were blinded by gold, and most of them couldn't see gold if it bit them on the nose. Gold was on every tongue, and it made some men mad. There was a madness about their disparate ambitions, their avidity, and their greedy hopes. They were united in Alaska by their callowness and their inexperience, qualities that frequently brought them to untimely, frozen ends.

Chilkoot Pass, Alaskan
gold rush, 1897.
Photographer unknown.

The chilling madness of this golden lust was symbolized by the famed Chilkoot Trail. It was not straight up, but it looked as though it were. It was a tortuous climb, but a single file of exhausted men was doggedly determined to reach the top. Over this frozen trail, each icy step painfully cut and even more painfully trod upon, lay the dream of gold. There was no alternative if one wished to reach the mines. The Chilkoot has come down to us in story and in legend so varied, so fanciful, so chillingly true it deserves little comment here. The photograph enshrines the disorganization, the chaotic, bizarre struggle of men against nature, a battle for nature's riches locked in the icebox to the north—Alaska.

143

As is true in every phase of the growth of America, its East, its West and finally its Northern Frontier, there were blacks who braved the circumstances and the difficulties of the problem to participate. Graphic proof of their participation in the struggle for Alaskan gold is this vignette.

In Alaska, as in every other frontier of the expanding United States, the fever of the gold rush finally abated. It was replaced with a calmer determination to build a livable country. Cities were needed, as well as industry and commerce, all the hallmarks of a stable, expanding venture. This blunt signpost "somewhere in Alaska" expresses the same resolve to build in that wild loneliness another human center. The sawn lumber in piles, the half-completed log cabin helped to clothe the dream in reality. Even the name, Klondyke City, heralds the birth of another commercial effort, another investment potential in capital-hungry Alaska.

Above:
Mining operation, Alaskan gold rush, 1898.
Photographer unknown.

Opposite page:
Dawson City, the Klondyke, 1898.
Photographer unknown.

And build they did. Alaskan towns and villages had certain characteristics in common with almost any other frontier center. Their signs were alike, wooden buildings were of the same mold, muddy streets were identical, everything looked interchangeable. But there were differences. Carts and wagons were drawn by Eskimo dogs, not by horses. Snow in patches on green hills was not an uncommon sight for many. The new arrivals needed to learn valuable lessons from the Eskimos, just as the immigrants moving into the Indian Southwest needed to depend on their hosts for lessons to help them live. Life among this gold-searching citizenry could be enthusiastic at times, and it was often symbolized by banners, signs, and flags whipping fiercely in brisk Alaskan breezes. No one *knew* where the gold was, so the search went on everywhere. Look at the flumes constructed to bring water for the waterwheels, the piles of slag, the rock that did not bear gold heaped in utter abandon. The mines and the miners lived cheek by jowl, and none were the better for it.

Opposite page:
Sawing timber for cabins and mine supports, Alaskan gold rush, 1898.
Photographer unknown.

Below:
Travel by dogsled, Alaskan gold rush, 1898.
Photographer unknown.

Demanding in its labor, absorbing in its consequences, the struggle against nature in the Alaskan wastes was endless. Machinery was lacking, skills were not adaptable to the conditions, but human energy was present in great abundance. So man reverted, as he must, to those lessons his forebears had learned painfully two hundred years before, and pitsawing, for example, was again in many cases, the only method for transforming trees into shelter for men. Eskimo dogs and primitive sleds were the only effective transport for men and goods in areas encrusted and covered with snow and ice. Unable to secure filet mignon and fine fish, the miner sustained his body with a steady diet of rough food. The reality of the Alaskan experience was symbolized by poor food and endless work, powered by driving ambition, and supported by fierce greed.

Miners at work, Alaskan gold rush, 1898.
Photographer unknown.

The common denominator of the Alaskan gold-bearing regions and the other frontier regions in the States was labor—hard, unceasing, physical labor. The hallmarks of the period, especially in Alaska, were shabby clothes and grueling, killing labor. The need for simple skills was almost overwhelming, and lessons learned a hundred years before were applied here in much the same form. It is a bit of a shock to see the rocker, developed for gold recovery in California in 1849, used again in identical fashion in 1898 in Alaska. Wooden flumes to bring badly needed water from the snow-covered mountains snaked through the Alaskan valleys for miles. Anything that could help the gold-recovery process was eagerly pressed into service. Nothing was too poor or too precious to serve the frantic search. The victim was the earth, and in time, man, as well, was required to bear the cost of this tragic, wanton ignorance.

Water flumes, Alaskan gold rush, 1898.
Photographer unknown.

Indians watch encroaching train,
Colorado, circa 1880.

The Native Americans

If symbols are needed as prototypes of the tragic Indian-white confrontation in the West, perhaps the most revealing is the railroad. These twin iron rails and the smoking Iron Horse that ran upon it delivered a death blow to the native Americans. Its tracks penetrated Indian lands everywhere, and they were followed by the white man in his many forms: settler, rancher, miner, farmer, and the hated army. Hard on their heels came speculators, land grabbers, Indian agents, preachers, merchants, and peace officers with their white man's law. There were more than enough white men who practiced the belief that "the only good Indian is a dead one." This thin snake of iron brought everything and everyone needed to doom the ways of life of most Indians. The symbol of irony is strong here as one blanket-wrapped Indian stares at the enemy high on the trestle while his companion turns away, one supposes in apprehension and disgust.

154

Among the most pitiable examples of human persistence was the struggle waged by many Indians in the more remote areas of the United States to maintain some semblance of their traditional life, however pressured, however abbreviated, however changed by the demands of an encroaching civiliza-tion that would not be stayed. Here in northern Wyoming we see Indians in their ancient splendor visited by a photographer. Frequently obliging, these Indians have dressed in clothes recalling other days, other victories, other splendors, an older life full of promise and meaning.

312

When these photographs were taken, in 1900, Chief
Wah-hah-yun-ta was the oldest living Indian. He was
born in 1781. The Chief once traveled to the national
Capitol where he was introduced to President Jefferson.
Photographer unknown.

Indian portraits taken in 1872.
Photographer, B. W. Kilburn.

A 128-year-old Hopi chief, circa 1880.
Photographer unknown.

Princess Angelina, Chief Seattle's daughter, circa 1890.
Photographer unknown.

Chief Sheet Lightning, circa 1890.
Photographer unknown.

Old skills were revered, treasured, and depended upon. They were not given up but maintained by old hands and old bodies recapturing old experiences, recalling the old excitement in memories of the golden yesterdays. Here the skilled construction of a tepee is demonstrated in its complexity by women, the traditional builders in the nomadic Indian tribes of the American Northwest.

Blackfoot Indians making tepee, northern Wyoming, circa 1902. *Photographer, N. A. Forsyth.*

Blackfoot squaw and children,
northern Wyoming, circa 1902.
Photographer, N. A. Forsythe.

Their relationship with nature was harmonious.
They used only what they needed, trying to maintain
the earth as they found it. Their religious beliefs supported such practices, and the simple structure of their
lives found its highest expression in such natural sur-
roundings as this lakeside in northern Wyoming. Unwilling prisoners in an industrial society they did not
understand, their stoic acceptance of the limited freedoms they enjoyed marks them for hallowed memory.
They feared no one man, yet the busy white world
taught them, and taught them savagely, that they
must beware of the land that had changed and the
new men who claimed to own the sacred earth.

Opposite page:
Salish Indian chief and family, northern
Montana, circa 1902.
Photographer, N. A. Forsyth.

This page:
Salish Indians, northern Montana, circa 1903.
Photographer, N. A. Forsyth.

The dwindling Indian world still included strong men of purpose. There were those who possessed the ability to face their persecutors with an indicting calm. They were fully aware that the white world pressed in upon them, recognizing that the days of another time, the olden days, were numbered. Look at this man's quiet passion, the implacable serenity with which he faces the photographer's camera. His very posture is a defense; his position as he stands is an assertion of confidence. This is where he belongs, in a setting expressing his character and his mode of life. The man and his environment complement each other and fittingly display the humanity that honest men find attractive forever.

Opposite page:
Hopi Indians, New Mexico, circa 1888.
Photographer, N. A. Forsyth.

Below:
Hopi Indians, New Mexico, circa 1888.
Photographer, N. A. Forsyth.

Far to the south there were other Indians pursuing an ancient way of life rooted in prehistory. They struggled to maintain themselves in the face of overt and bitter persecution by the U.S. Bureau of Indian Affairs. The life of these Indians enshrined the simple but enduring skills of basketry, weaving, pottery, and religious devotions. Living on rocky mesas high above the desert floor, their daily existence was hard and limited in pleasures. Yet it provided a bare subsistence, offering a richness of human relationships that has endured, finding acceptance among some whites as a viable pattern for white society.

Above:
Hopi Indian weaving blanket, New Mexico, circa 1888.
Photographer unknown.

Opposite page:
Hopi Indians, New Mexico, circa 1888.
Photographer unknown.

Working under the most primitive conditions on handmade looms, Hopi Indians have skillfully produced blankets and carpets of unsurpassed excellence. Reflecting traditional as well as ancient designs embodying totemic symbols meaningful only to their originators, Hopi blankets have found their place in the history of fine weaving. The Hopi Indians, almost unknown and unsung, live today in the harsh circumstances required of them as unwilling wards of an inconsiderate and uncaring government.

The Hopi way of life embodies deep religious devotion and participation including Snake dances, Corn dances, and Antelope dances. It requires religious idols, handmade, painted objects called Kachinas. Based on ancient foods and ancient remedies, it is a way of living needing few of the artificial supports characteristic of contemporary white life. The Hopi maintain the skills of their fathers with quiet and dignified determination. The products they make for their living needs have transformed their simple living

requirements into collectors' pieces and art objects of great worth. The Hopi's fate, the ignominy and obscurity of their lives, remains a social cancer; indifference to it must be tolerated no longer.

Hopi girls weaving baskets,
New Mexico, circa 1888.
Photographer unknown.

Hopi woman making pottery,
New Mexico, 1884.
Photographer unknown.

Most highly prized of Hopi skills are the ancient arts of pottery making. Here is a skilled Hopi woman, the traditional pottery maker, using coils of wetted clay to create a pot. It will be fired, but only after it has been beautifully painted by hand with one of the traditional religious symbols so prized and revered by these peaceful people. Eventually and perhaps, finally, it will find its way as a high-priced commodity in private hands, traded and sold, back and forth between collectors. The works of these largely unknown artisans have been firmly established as significant works of American art, occupying important positions in museum collections. The irony is that such valuable social artifacts are produced by a people uncared for, mistreated, and exploited, living out their short lives in virtual obscurity on a waterless mesa high above the parched desert.

Navaho Indian family in front of their hogan, 1882.
Photographer unknown.

For many Navajos, a larger, neighboring tribe of the Hopi, life has moved them closer to the accepted white image of an assimilated Indian. From the earliest days, in which they lived as roving nomads in hogans such as the one shown here, their lives have changed much. Effective and prolonged legal and public pressure on the U.S. government has produced for the Navajos a larger share of the income from the land that was always theirs. This newfound wealth has enabled them to organize a different style of life for themselves, and time will indicate more fully how helpful this has been. The unyielding conflict of cultures that constitutes the relationships of Indians to whites and to the dominant white institutions remains in force, still to be reconciled for the benefit of all.

Chief White Eagle of the Sauk
tribe, circa 1880.
Photographer unknown.

Enlargement showing U.S. Cavalry revolver and belt buckle.
Partially obscured is a set of framed photographs.

There are two perplexing items in this splendid photograph of a Sauk family outside their summer dwelling in the Minnesota forests. First there is no apparent explanation why the Indian man wears in his belt, a U.S. Army issue, a framed daguerreotype of a white settler family of three. One would assume such an object was not normally the prized property of a nomadic Indian nor the kind of possession that might have interested him in any sense. Again, one can only wonder where the Colt revolver with holster might have come from, particularly when there seems to be no ammunition handy. Could it be that these are the tools of the trade, the "props" the photographer carried with him to make the kind of picture he thought he could sell?

In the painful process of assimilation, there were those individuals in every tribe who fought determinedly to maintain the practices, the rites, the skills, and the activities of their youth. This Indian finds solace and comfort smoking his pipe while the meat of slain animals dries in the sun. This product, called *jerky* by white men, was essential for nourishment in the long, snowy winters when game was light, hunting difficult, and the needed government issue of meat was late. Promised solemnly in treaty obligations, delivery of beef was uncertain and often of poor or dubious nutritional value. A strange paradox is offered in the hooped wagon by the tepee, a type once widely used to bring the white settler, the Indians' hated trespasser. Used by the Indians, it served for transport where once there was the dog-drawn travois or the fleet pony.

Salish Indians, northern Montana, 1903.
Photographer, N. A. Forsyth.

Indian respect for ancient traditions passed away very slowly. Some vestiges of it hung on stubbornly, and it was not hard to find examples of the young learning the old ways. This photograph reveals the seriousness with which even the youngest of the children undertook to share in the ancient rites. It was clearly evident that if the old ways were to survive, the young needed to uphold and defend the rich heritage. Under attack by government agents, the churches, and those Indians who were anxious to become "white red men," the old ways were diminishing in prestige among some sections of the tribes. As the old religious rites were suppressed by the Bureau of Indian Affairs and frequently strictly forbidden in some areas, Indians developed subtle devices for participating both in the white man's religion and their own ancient devotions. For a nation founded on the principles of religious freedom, steeped in the strictest separation of the church and state, this photograph is a special reminder of the inhumanity with which Indians viewed the deprivation of their religious freedoms.

Above:
Salish Indians, northern Montana, 1903.
Photographer, N. A. Forsyth.

Opposite page:
Salish Indians, northern Montana, 1903.
Photographer, N. A. Forsyth.

Plains Indians, circa 1901.
Photographer, N. A. Forsyth.

Searching endlessly for a way out of the blind alleys in which they increasingly found themselves, the older Indians sang and danced, appealing to spirits that had provided help in the great years behind them. They were puzzled by the bewildering legal, political tangle that characterized their relationship with the government, and they tried to provide effective leadership for their people. Deceived and confused, their comfort lay in maintaining rites and activities, dances and songs that had brought aspiration, meaning, and joy to the people in days gone by. They danced and sang as long as they could and tried to inspire and teach the young to follow in their faltering footsteps.

Plains Indians, circa 1901.
Photographer, N. A. Forsyth.

190

For certain Indians there were deep pleasures and unspoken satisfactions in dressing in the regalia of the better days, recalling an active life that had purpose and meaning. Even for white photographers, these old men were symbols of a different kind and were accorded a special respect and consideration.

This brutal conflict between reverence for the old ways by some Indians and contempt for the old on the part of many who witnessed ancient ceremonials was a crushing blow. It marked the acceleration of the end, the last pitiful days of a fading, degrading relationship between Indian and white.

Above:
Salish Indians, northern Montana, 1903.
Photographer, N. A. Forsyth.

Opposite page:
Plains Indians, circa 1901.
Photographer, N. A. Forsyth.

191

Indian portrait, 1872.
Photographer, B. W. Kilburn.

Tired, worn out, defeated at last, some Indians were employed as models by frontier photographers. They were feeble examples of the Indians the settlers had learned to fear and to respect as antagonists. Secure in the belief that the Plains Indians were conquered, no longer a threat, no longer able to defend their lands and their families, frontier photographers avidly produced acceptable pictures of the cowed

Indian. Such pictures of Indian models had little to do with Indian life. They brought pity for the subjects and dishonor to those who used their victimized condition for their own gain. So the old Indian vanished, to be replaced, in time, by a new breed of Indian, finding useful molds in which to recreate the image of their forefathers, the proud and able Indian men and women of nineteenth-century America.

Indian portrait, 1882.
Photographer, Joseph E. Smith.

5

The Bountiful Land

Many of the immigrants who came to the United States were farmers or members of families that had been farmers. They were men and women who valued the land, and it was the land above all that they desired. They wished to settle it, to own it, to till it, to reap its harvest, to glory in the security it afforded and the satisfaction and the pride it engendered. For years they gave the land their labor, their devotion, and their love; they gave under conditions of great physical stress, loneliness, isolation, and difficulty beyond our ability to describe adequately or recall anymore. The labor was the labor of the hands, the arms, the backs, and the stout legs. This photograph is a monument to the many farmers who sowed and reaped by hand and expected little else but God's blessings and a reasonable profit for their labors. Such were the men and women who came to the West to transform it into a blooming and fruitful wonderland.

Oklahoma farmers, 1895.
Photographer unknown.

It was no wonder that harvest time was celebrated or that both photographer and subject saw point in recording such a happy event. It was no wonder that the size of these pumpkins was just cause for an expression of joy and delight. It was no wonder at all that a beaming young lady shared the great satisfaction of the three farmers who loaded nature's bounty into the farm wagon.

Wheat harvesting,
Walla Walla, Washington, circa 1890.
Photographer unknown.

There came a time when it was beyond the ability of men, with the puny power of only their arms and their bodies, to accomplish the goals that were set for the farmers of the entire nation. The abundance of crops that was needed required machinery, and machinery came. It was the utilization of this machinery that transformed the farmer from a workman into something approaching a sailor of the land. One can visualize the similarities between the swooping of a ship upon the blue ocean and the up-and-down course of a forty-horse team. Over waving fields of wheat, endless in their configuration, up and down, over and around, with nothing but wheat fields, the land, and the blue sky to bless their labors, the similarity is believable, indeed.

Wheat harvesting,
Walla Walla, Washington, circa 1890.
Photographer unknown.

It is well not to become so devoted to machines that one fails to remember that in the end machines must be run and controlled by the men who created them. It was these stolid farmers' skills, their inherited intuitive understanding of the weather and the earth, their recognition of the many danger signs of nature, the signs of growth and the signs of decay on which their success depended. These men, browned, hardened, tough, and incommunicative, were the machine

tenders. They brought to the fields and to the machines they served the labor needed to make them productive. These were true Midwestern heroes. These men and their women and children provided the one essential ingredient without which there would have been no growth. That is, of course, the understanding, the devotion, the aspiration, and the inspiration that only men can bring to labor.

Wheat farming, Nebraska, circa 1900.
Photographer unknown.

Baling hay, Nebraska, circa 1890.
Photographer unknown.

The work was interminable. Where machinery was available, it was effectively used. More than that, it was improved. And where there was none, the ancient methods sufficed as they had for thousands of years. Together man and machine provided the bountiful crops on which the nation grew and on which the faraway places of the world depended more and more.

Western Kansas wheat farmers, circa 1910.
Photographer unknown.

Opposite page, above:
Harvest time, western Kansas, circa 1900.
Photographer unknown.

Below:
Sundown harvest of wheat in western Kansas, circa 1890.
Photographer unknown.

There was the frequently unnoticed graphic side of farming—the labor, the heat, the dust, and the sweat. They provided pictures of unending excitement and dramatic pleasure—the loneliness of the prairie, the piled high character of the wheat, the exhausted men pausing to drink sweet, cold water. These were all part of the products, the by-products if you will, of the energies of labor required to subdue the land and bring it to heel for the needs of a growing mankind.

Candid photograph of midwestern father and daughter, circa 1890.
Photographer unknown.

This endless labor provided one other precious ingredient; it provided leisure, a new quality in life. A quality that was known only in the Old Country to the titled and the well-to-do. When the dream of America was realized, it allowed a family to find the time, the location, and the means to indulge in pleasures formerly denied them completely. The opportunity to gather in concord to sing, to pray, to gaze upon nature, to eat well, to dress well, to enjoy the esteem of their neighbors—this was the dream, the realization for people that labor and machinery brought to the Middle West of America.

Leavenworth church group,
Leavenworth, Kansas, circa 1905.
Photographer unknown.

The pleasures to be derived from leisure were not always so formal, not always so grandiose. There was the simple pleasure of rest from labor, as well as the ability to sit on one's own porch secure in the knowledge that a little portion of the world, one's own precious castle, was his and hers. There was the pleasure of holding growing children and knowing that their future looked secure. The recognition that one's own labor had provided the expected reward was good. The promise inherent in the dream of America and in the dream of God had come to pass, and life was rich, as it was supposed to be.

Nebraska family, circa 1890.
Photographer, Silas Melander.

Repairing streets, San Francisco,
California, circa 1900.
Photographer unknown.

Cities grew quickly but not as planned instruments of beauty and order. Rather, they grew helter-skelter and randomly. It was as though there was not the time required to build the city, and yet, the cities had to be built. Men labored; they tore up streets and replaced them; they made new streets. Telephone lines were strung from tall poles erected in the streets, and all was done in seemingly the same breath. The cities reinforced everyone's belief that the grand dreams had no limits. There was no end to the activities of labor that were needed to transform the plains of the West. Few people foresaw the crush, the crowding, the fencing in, the destruction of nature that would follow. It was a time for building, not for criticizing.

Unidentified Colorado town, circa 1890.
Photographer unknown.

213

Texas oil town, circa 1900.
Photographer unknown.

And the earth responded, almost as though there had been a signed agreement of partnership. The land opened and produced natural rewards man could not have dreamed of. Not the least of these was black gold, petroleum. Oil could, and did, transform the earth itself: revolutionizing machinery, transforming technologies, adding dimensions to the world that were near-frightening to ponder. Towns created by the rush to mine this new liquid gold rivaled gold-rush villages in sprawl and splendor. In nineteenth-century Midwestern America oil derricks and power lines were as plentiful as covered wagons and oxen had been seventy-five years before.

Early motorists, 1905.
Photographer unknown.

One of the greatest blessings provided by the discovery of petroleum was the gasoline engine and the many vehicles it powered. Frightening horses, raising unanswered questions in the minds of many, the automobile stubbornly fought for and won its rightful place in an emerging technological society. Limited at first to the well-to-do, the automobile, under the genius of Henry Ford, soon became available in larger quantities to those with lesser incomes. It was purchased by all who could possibly afford it. In time it became as common to see automobiles in various emergency conditions on the primitive roads as it had formerly been to see horses and buggies, oxen and wagons plodding their way slowly across the self-same trails.

Early motorist, 1905.
Photographer unknown.

Nature was not always cooperative to the new, gasoline-powered animal. It was as though there was a tacit understanding between them that each could do its own thing, not in concord but in conflict. For when it rained and the roads were muddy, the progress of the automobile was increasingly difficult. Chains for tires were developed to ease the problem, and every type of gadget was hopefully attached to cars to overcome this obstacle to mechanical progress. But in the end, all it produced was a greater resolve to build roads that would not become a sea of mud. The search led to macadam and to asphalt and only then were the great possibilities for maintaining dependable highways for gasoline-powered vehicles fully realized.

Following page:
Early motorists stop to repair tire, 1905.
Photographer unknown.

Chicago-Saint Paul Automotive Race, 1905.
Photographer unknown.

The structural weaknesses of man-made things was, and has remained, a plague to weary mankind. Everyone seemed to share the hopeful expectation that mechanical devices would last forever, but it became clear in the case of the automobile that this was untrue. For in spite of man's best efforts, automobiles and their many parts broke down and always at the worst time. Once again, as in this photograph, the age-old power of muscles, blocks, and tackles came to the rescue of the machine, and unhappily in the middle of an auto race from Chicago to St. Paul in 1905.

Automobiles soon became vehicles for conducting the most ordinary activities. For instance, hunting was made easier because the automobile could bring the hunter and his equipment almost to the scene of the hunt. Visiting, which was enshrined in the buggy, became the property of the limousine, the sedan, and the touring car. And the young, when afforded the opportunity, were as much of a nuisance with their cars as they are today.

Motorcyclist, early 1900s.
Photographer unknown.

It was inevitable that someone would put an engine on the bicycle. They did, ushering in the era of the motorcycle. For those who could not afford four wheels, two wheels became an accepted mode of transportation, and it produced a new look, a new set of clothes, and a new attitude. Goggles, cap worn backwards, heavy leather gloves, and something around the legs to protect them from the hot engine became the accepted costume of the motorcyclist. Names like Indian and Harley-Davidson became "in" words among those young enough and daring enough to accept the risks involved in riding the early motorcycles.

Automobile repair, 1905.
Photographer unknown.

The automobile made it possible to link the cities to the countryside more easily and firmly, both for commerce and for visiting. In addition to bringing people to and from the city, these gasoline-powered vehicles transformed the cities themselves. The automobile and the bus upgraded the city dweller's ability to function, to get around, and to live in new, time-saving fashions. Buses, charabancs, delivery trucks, roadsters, and other self-powered vehicles, were popular aids in helping immigrants trying to find new life patterns in the emerging cities.

State Street, Chicago, Illinois, early 1900s.
Photographer unknown.

Residential street scene, circa 1920.
Photographer unknown.

Soon it became necessary to consider building a previously unknown appendage for many homes, a driveway. These early driveways sloped from the rear of the house to the street, were cast of concrete, and featured a shelter for the automobile called a garage.

There the gleaming beast could be protected from wind, weather, and the dirty hands of mischievous boys and girls. The driveway added a new hazard to the demands of everyday living. One needed to be aware of and watch out for cars backing out of drive-

Man's attempt to fly, circa 1900.
Photographer unknown.

ways. Having created the means to move rapidly on city streets with gasoline engines, man turned his attention to the art of flying. The early twentieth-century was witness to serious, intelligent, foolish, and downright dangerous attempts to master the art of living in the air and flying through it. The foolhardy attempt of the early experimenter seen here was doomed to disappointment and maybe a broken leg or two for the hardy aeronaut.

Technical Appendix

Good photographic print quality with excellent overall image definition and optimum tone range, black and white, can be obtained from original early positive or negative material. The restoration of the original daguerreotype, tintype, or glass or nitrate film negative involves problems unique to each item and therefore cannot be discussed in general terms. But once the negative has been prepared, and barring special problems—which unfortunately are common—I have been able to make good prints from seemingly unprintable glass negatives and daguerreotypes by maintaining close control of negative density readings with a transmission densitometer and by using different equipment, light sources, chemistry, and lenses.

Although the printing treatment for each original glass negative is different, good results usually may be achieved with the following equipment, materials, methods, and procedures.

• ENLARGERS

Print contrast and image sharpness can be raised or lowered according to the negative by using an enlarger with a cold light source for low contrast and a point light source with condensers for high contrast and sharp image.

Caesar Saltzman enlarger 8 x 10 converted to 11 x 14 negative accommodation. Point light source. Mercury vapor. Condenser system with point light and 500-watt enlarging bulb #302. Aristo Grid light.

Omega D-2 enlarger 4 x 5, with point light source and condensers. Enlarging bulb #212 with variable condenser system.

5 x 7 E-3 Omega enlarger with cold light source.

5 x 7 Durst 138S enlarger with point light source and Aristo Grid cold light.

• ENLARGING LENSES

Schneider Componon	2X Plan Achromat Nikon
Nikon El Nikkor	3X Plan Achromat Nikon
Nikon Macro Nikkor	4X Plan Achromat Nikon
Rodenstock Rodagon	10X Plan Achromat Nikon
1.2 Plan Achromat Nikon	C.P. Goerz Apochromat Artars

• PHOTOMICROGRAPHIC SYSTEMS (used on a vibration eliminator base)
Nikon Multiphot   Nikon Microflex Model AFM used on a Nikon Microscope

• ILLUMINATION & FILTERING

For transmission negative enlarging: collimated light; Kohler illumination, central, oblique, and dark field illumination.

To copy with Panchromatic film, place a #58 Eastman green filter in the light path.

To copy daguerreotypes and tintypes, place polarization filters over the copy lights and the camera lens to vary the degree of reflection and shadow detail.

• PHOTOGRAPHIC PRINTING PAPERS AND FILMS

Eastman Poly Contrast Rapid Enlarging paper	Eastman Commercial film #6127
AGFA Brovira photographic enlarging paper	Eastman Contrast Process Ortho film #4154
Eastman Professional Copy film #4.25	Eastman Masking film
Eastman Super XX Pan film #4142	

• CONTACT PRINTING AND PAPER
Morse Contact printer with argon light source
Eastman AZO contact printing paper
Contact prints are also made under the enlarger with enlarging paper

• FILM DEVELOPER
Eastman HC110, Eastman D-19, Eastman DK-50, Eastman D-11, Eastman DK-60, Eastman D-76, Eastman D-23, Windisch.

• PAPER DEVELOPER & HYPO
Eastman Dektol diluted 2 water 1 developer stock solution
Eastman Dektol diluted 3 water 1 developer stock solution
Eastman Dektol diluted 6 water 1 developer stock solution
Eastman Selectol and Selectol Soft with Dektol as second developer
Eastman Rapid Fix Hypo bath

• BLEACHING
To bleach: use a solution of 10-20 grains of potassium ferricyanide in 8 ounces of water and apply to the print with a cotton swab; then the print is dipped in a hypo bath, with a contrast tone reduction. Test the bleaching on a discarded print for strength of bleach.
To bleach without losing contrast: use 10-20 grains of ammonium persulphate in 1 ounce of water. Apply to the local area of the print with cotton.

Index

Note: Boldface numbers indicate material that appears in photos or captions.